CHEROKEE TONE

CWY SZBEA

JW WEBSTER

CONTENTS

1.0 LAYOUT
1.1 TONE MARKING

In Cherokee words, vowels carry length and tone—consonants do not. Therefore, in this guidebook--tone marking is placed above each vowel using my own adaptation of the number system that was presented in the Cherokee-English Dictionary, DF.

If the vowel is a short syllable—a single numeral representation of the tone is placed above that vowel.
E.g. na^2, 'that'

If the vowel is long syllable—the numeral tone representation is doubled and placed above that vowel.
E.g. tsi^{22}sdu^2, 'rabbit'
(The first syllable is long and the second is pronounced short)

Using the number system to mark tone and length, it is much easier to read the word more accurately by allowing tone and length to be presented together in the same area apart from the syllables themselves.

1.2 ASPIRATION

All aspirated consonants are marked by a preceding /h/.
E.g. hy, hl, etc.

Aspirated vowels (a, e, i, o, u, v) are represented by the
syllabary characters ha, he, hi, ho, hu, and hv.

1.3 SILENT CHARACTERS

In this guidebook, all silent vowels are marked with a superscript 0 (^{0}).
E.g. go^{22}hwe^{22}li^2 'book' is frequently pronounced with the final vowel /i/
dropped and to show this vowel deletion—a superscript 0 is marked
as shown below.

E.g. go^{22}hwe^{22}li^0 ᎪᏪᏟ

2.0 CHEROKEE TONES

2.1 Level Tones:

(1) low
(2) mid or default
(3) high
(4) derivational tone or super-high

2.2 Contour Tones:

(23) rising
(32) falling
(21) low-fall
(11) low (derivational)

Did you know that you already use Cherokee tones when you speak English?
Below are isolated examples of the same tones used in English intonation.

2.3 Level Tone Cognates

(1)   u^{11}h... (when thinking)
(2)   I^{2}t's
(3)   Wha^{33}t??
(4)   No^4! (when aggravated)

2.4 Contour Tone Cognates

(21) Da^{21}ng! (unsympathetic/sarcastic)
(23) Ri^{23}ght?
(32) Ri^{32}ght!

2.5 English Sentences (With Tone Marking)

1) I^2 ca^{22}n't be^{2}lie^{32}ve he^2 di^{22}d tha^{2}t!
2) I^{2}s tha^{2}t fo^{2}r me^{23}?

2.6 Yes! You Already Use Cherokee Tones

Below are examples of single English words and by altering their tones (intonation) the expressed meanings are changed.

Ye^{2}s	neutral;uninterested
Ye^{32}s	positive response; 'I agree'
Ye^{23}s	question;eliciting a response
Ye^{34}s	disappointment;'Is it a yes??'
Ye^{44}s	aggravated; irritated response
Ye^{3223}s	carry on; 'I'm listening...'
Ye^{2332}s	reserved; indicating doubt

2.7 Frequency

Some tones occur more frequently than others.

> (2) most common tone (default)
> (3) very common (-o³³ʔi, -e³³ʔi)
> (4) not very common (derivational tone)
>
> ga¹¹na³ʔli² 'castrated animal'
> ga¹¹na⁴⁴li² 'lazy'
> ga²du³ 'on top'
> ga⁴⁴du³ 'bread'
>
> (21) common
> (a²¹gi²-, 'first person pronoun'/ -sgo²¹, 'question suffix')
> (23) very common **(only occurs on long vowels)**
> (32) very common **(only occurs on long vowels)**

2.8 Derivational or Super-High Tone (4)

Rule: The super-high tone (4) is only found on the right-most long vowel of a word.
Examples:

> 1) a⁴ʔdv³, 'young animal' (litter/hatched)
> 2) a²ʔni⁴⁴dv³, 'young animals'
> 3) e⁴⁴gwa³, 'large'
> 4) wa²hya²ni⁴⁴dv⁰, 'Young Wolf'

In (1) and (3) above, another rule is governing over the rule that states the (4) tone can only be found on the right-most long vowel of a word. Since (1) and (3) above are both two syllable words consisting of short syllables--the (4) tone is placed on the first syllable of the word because the governing rule states that Cherokee words cannot end with long syllables.

2.9 Practicing Tone Application

The examples below have the same number of syllables in both Cherokee and English. Practice saying each English translation with the Cherokee tones that correspond with each syllable.

1) He^{3}llo^2! Ho^{22}w a^{33}re yo^{2}u
si^{3}yo^2 to^{22}hi^{33}tsu^2

2) I^{22}t's ju^{23}st fi^{2}ne.
o^{22}si^{23}gwu^2

3) me^{22}di^{32}ci^{2}ne
nv^{22}wo^{32}ti^2

2.10 Examples of Cherokee Tone

(11) low-falling tone: (occurs only on long vowels)
sv^{11}gi^{2}, 'onion' ko^{11}sdu^{2}, 'ashes'

(2) mid/default tone: (occurs on long or short vowels)
long vowel: yv^{22}gi^{2}, 'fork' short vowel: a^{2}le^{3}, 'and'

(3) high tone: (occurs on long or short vowels)
long: ge^{33}ga^{2}, 'I'm going' short: i^{2}tse^{3}(^{3}ʔi^{2}) 'new'

(4) derivational/super-high tone (occurs only on long vowels)
i^{2}yu^{44}sdi^{0}, 'like' e^{44}gwa^{2}, 'large'

(23) rising: (occurs only on long vowels)
e^{23}ha^{2}, 'she/he's living' ko^{23}la^{2}, 'bone'

(32) falling tone: (occurs only on long vowels)
ge^{23}do^{32}ʔa^{2}, 'I'm going around'
a^{21}li^{0}sda^{32}yv^{0}hv^{3}sga^{2}, 'She/he's eating a meal'

3.0 PRONUNCIATION GUIDE

3.1 VOWELS:

3.1 VOWELS:	Ꭰ,	Ꭱ,	Ꭲ,	Ꭳ,	Ꭴ,	Ꭵ
Phonetic:	a,	e,	i,	o,	u,	v
Pronunciation	awe	ay	ee	oh	oo	uh

3.2 CONSONANTS

The consonants stem from the six vowels shown above. Presented below are the consonants and how they are pronounced with the vowels. For those sounds that have a corresponding English example, those words are presented with parentheses around the part of the word that contains the Cherokee sound. For other sounds that did not have a corresponding English equivalent, a simple "sounds like" example has been given.

Ꭶ (go)ne	Ꭸ (gue)ss			Ꭹ s(ki)	Ꭺ go	Ꭻ goo	Ꭼ (gu)
Ꭽ (ha)ll	Ꭾ (hea)vy			Ꭿ he	Ꮀ hoe	Ꮁ who	Ꮂ (hu)nt
Ꮃ law	Ꮄ (le)ver			Ꮅ lee	Ꮆ low	Ꮇ Lou	Ꮈ (lu)ck
Ꮉ (Mo)lly	Ꮊ (me)t			Ꮋ me	Ꮌ mow	Ꮍ moo	
Ꮎ (no)t	Ꮏ hnaw	Ꮐ na	Ꮑ (ne)t	Ꮒ knee	Ꮓ no	Ꮔ new	Ꮕ (nu)t
Ꮖ (qua)ntity	Ꮗ kweh			Ꮘ kwee	Ꮙ (quo)te	Ꮚ kwoo	Ꮛ kwuh
Ꮜ (sa)w	Ꮞ (se)t			Ꮟ see	Ꮠ sew	Ꮡ sue	Ꮢ (su)m
Ꮣ (do)ll	Ꮥ (de)bt			Ꮧ dee	Ꮩ doe	Ꮪ due	Ꮫ (du)ck
Ꮭ tlaw	Ꮮ tleh			Ꮯ Quie(tly)	Ꮰ tlow	Ꮱ tloo	Ꮲ tluh
Ꮳ jaw	Ꮴ jay			Ꮵ jee	Ꮶ (jo)ke	Ꮷ (Ju)ne	Ꮸ (ju)nk
Ꮹ (wa)ll	Ꮺ (we)st			Ꮻ we	Ꮼ (wo)'nt	Ꮽ wou)nd	Ꮾ (wha)t
Ꮿ (yo)nder	Ᏸ (ye)s			Ᏹ (yie)ld	Ᏺ (yol)k	Ᏻ you	Ᏼ (yu)ck

3.3 Special Sounds Due To Vowel Deletion

hw,	as (wh) in cool <u>wh</u>ip "Stewie Griffin"
hy,	as (hu) in hue, huge, and human
khk,	as in (ckg) in ba<u>ckg</u>round

de³³ki⁰gi²²lo³³ʔa²,   'he/she is washing (flexible items)'

ks,	as (x) in ta<u>x</u>

tsu²²ka⁰sv²³sdi²   'smoke'

kd	as (ckd) in ba<u>ckd</u>oor

kv⁰di³ha²   'he/she is using it'

kt	as (ckt) in qui<u>ck t</u>urn

sv²²ka⁰ta²   'apple'

skw,	as (squ) in <u>squ</u>ander and square

squu³   'too/also'

dl	as (dl) in col<u>d l</u>ast night

a²²dla²   'rubber'

ts	as (ts) in cu<u>ts </u>and ligh<u>ts</u>
tskw	as (tsqu) in qui<u>t squ</u>awking
ʔ	This symbol represents a (glottal stop). This is when you are speaking and the sound is abruptly cut off and then you continue speaking again.

English example: Uh-oh!

The soundless space between (Uh) and (oh) is known as a
glottal stop.

4.0 TONE & VERB PARTS

The Cherokee verb consists of the following parts in consecutive order;

[Prepronoun Prefix + Pronoun + Root + Root Suffix + Aspect + Tense Suffix + Additional Modifiers]

Example:

Prepronoun	Pronoun	Root	Root Suffix	Aspect	Tense Suffix	Modifiers
w(i)	$i^{21}di^{22}$	hya^2l	h	$i^{23}do^{32}h$	$v^{23}ʔi^2$	Ø

$wi^{21}di^{22}hya^2(h)li^{23}do^{32}hv^{23}ʔi^2$ We were looking for it from place to place there.

The sections above that are shaded in light grey have PREDICTABLE tone and the Root Suffix is also predictable but they are comprised of consonants and consonants do not carry tone. Only vowels carry tone.

What is of interest is that when these morphemes (word parts) join together, they can create tone changes that can seem difficult but are not as complex as one might think.

Prepronoun's That Cause Tone Change:

de^{33} (verbal pluralizer)   The (^{33}) tone can spread rightward but only onto long vowels. If the following vowel is short, the (^{33}) tone will stay on the prepronoun /de/. The tone also cannot spread rightward if that vowel is already a (^{33}) tone.

Tone Shift: $de^{22}ga^{33}so^2hga^2$ she/he is crossing water

No Tone Shift: $de^{33}ga^{33}tli^{22}si^{23}ha^2$ she/he is gathering them

$de^{33}ga^2no^{22}tsa^2tlv^3sga^2$ she/he is advertising

11

i^{22}y(xx)^{33} (quantity/quality)　　This prefix will always cause the following vowel to raise to a (33) tone.

i^{22}yu^{33}wa^{44}gu^{0}hdi^{2}　　(how ever many) times

i^{22}yu^{33}de^{22}ti^{2}yv^{44}dv^{2}　　(how ever many) years

Modifier's (Clitics) That Cause Tone Change

Remember: all (3) tones must be long syllables. Due to this, any suffix modifier that is a (3) tone will cause the previous vowel to take one of the (3) tones which causes a rising tone.

tsa^{2}yo^{33}si^{23}ha^{2}　　you are hungry

tsa^{2}yo^{33}si^{23}tsu^{3}　　Are you hungry?

Here, the (ha) syllable has been deleted to allow the rising syllable to connect to the question modifier. This is possible because we still know that this is present tense because of the stem form.

In summary, prepronoun prefixes and suffix modifiers are the only verb parts that cause tone change.

5.0 TONE & INTONATION

In English, intonation is used to convey emotion or importance of context. For example, English speakers can use intonation to place emphasis on a single word in an utterance to show that is has more importance. Test this for yourself by placing intonation on the single word in **bold** below.

The big red, car.

The **big**, red car.

The big, **red** car.

The big, red **car**.

This is a feature of English that does not exist in Cherokee. Due to the fact that Cherokee is a tonal language, we cannot allow anything to interfere with the tone of a word or the meaning can either be modified or rendered meaningless. Tone is a crucial aspect to the speaking and understanding of Cherokee. In English you could say the word "car" with multiple forms of intonation or pitch changes and everyone will still know that you are saying "car". This is not possible in many tonal languages, including Cherokee.

If we don't use intonation the same as English speakers—how do we use intonation? In Cherokee, we use suffix modifier's to convey intonation and we use root suffixes for conveying focus of the action.

5.1 Suffix Modifier's

$wu^3(^3\text{ʔi}^2)$ Suffix used for emphasizing a particular word

         E.g. $o^{44}sdv^2wu^3(^3\text{ʔi}^2)$ It is just good.

dv^{33} Suffix used to mean "definitely"

         E.g. $o^{44}sdv^2dv^{33}$ It is definitely good.

5.2 Root Suffixes

h　　　(horizontal) motion focus

　　　E.g.　$u^{22}le^2$**h**di^2　　for one to stand　(focus is on the motion of the action)

ʔ　　　vertical motion/stationary focus

　　　E.g.　$a^{21}de^{22}hlo^0hgwa^3$**ʔ**a^2　　she/he is learning

　　　　　　　　　　　　　　　　　　(focus is on the fact that no movement is

　　　　　　　　　　　　　　　　　　visible in the action itself)

　　　E.g.　ga^2de^{33}**ʔ**a^2　　she/he is removing a hanging object

　　　　　　　　　　　　　　　　　　(focus is on the vertical motion of the action)

s　　　subject focus

　　　E.g.　$u^{22}yo^{22}hu^{22}$**s**$v^{23}ʔi^2$　　she/he died

　　　　　　　　　　　　　　　　　　(focus is on the subject or the person that died)

g　　　object focus

　　　E.g.　$a^{11}dli^{32}$**g**a^2　　she/he is pouring it

　　　　　　　　　　　　　　　　　　(focus is on the object or the thing being poured)

sg　　　subject/object focus

　　　E.g.　$a^{21}di^{23}ta^3$**sg**a^2　　she/he is drinking it

　　　　　　　　　　　　　　　　　　(focus is on the fact that the subject is drinking it)

ts　　　finalized/completed focus

　　　E.g.　$u^{21}yo^{33}$**ts**$v^{23}ʔi^2$　　she/he became spoiled

　　　　　　　　　　　　　　　　　　(focus is on the finalized state of the subject)

Note: This root suffix is mostly found on verbs that use the transformative conditional suffix as part of the compounded root.

n   not a true root suffix because it comes from the populative infix /ahn/

E.g.   du²¹lv²³hwi⁰sda¹¹**ne**²³ha²   she/he is working

d(e),   verbal pluralizer

u,   Set B (personal experience) pronoun

lvhwisd,   to thwart   incorporated infinitive   s= subject focus

    di= infinitive tense suffix

ahn,   populative infix   used on most incorporated infinitive verb forms

eh,   applicative conditional suffix in its incompletetive stem form

a,   present tense suffix

Ø   this means that the root does not have a suffix and is found on the immediate stem

E.g.   ha²di²³ta²   Drink it!

Note: The immediate stem generally does not have a root suffix because root suffixes are used to classify action. A command is not "real" action and this is why it cannot be classified with a root suffix.

6.0 EXPRESSING TONE IN WRITTEN CHEROKEE

Linguists have described the creation of new words or new verbs as "derivation", and what this means is that the noun root or verb root is undergoing a tone change in order to convert the original root to a new meaning or to change the word class entirely, i.e. when a verb root is converted to an adjective, adverb, etc.

We will first look at some examples of derivation and how they are formed. I will give the examples according to which stem form they are derived from and discuss the changes that are made in order to reflect the new "derived" meaning. Secondly, we will look at how these tone changes are reflected in syllabary writing.

Incompletive Stem Derivations

a^{21}dle^{33}sgv^{23}ʔi^2 one was turning off (verb)
    a^{22}dle^{33}sgv^{44}ʔi^2 a turn off (noun)

- The pronoun switches from (^{21}) "realistic" to (^{22}) "unrealistic.
- The rightmost long vowel increased from (^{23}) "past tense" to (^{44}) "any time"

a^{21}do^{33}ni^{22}sgv^{23}ʔi^2 one was talking to themselves (verb)
    a^{22}do^{33}ni^{44}sgi^2 sorcerer (noun)
      This is reflecting the observation that medicine people appear to be whispering to themselves when they are reciting medicine verses.

- The pronoun switches from (^{21}) "realistic" to (^{22}) "unrealistic.
- The rightmost long vowel increased from (^{23}) "past tense" to (^{44}) "any time"

a^{21}de^{33}yo^{2}hv^{23}ʔi^2 one was going around a curve (verb)
    a^{22}de^{33}yo^{2}hv^{44}ʔi^2 a curve (noun)
- The pronoun switches from (^{21}) "realistic" to (^{22}) "unrealistic.
- The rightmost long vowel increased from (^{23}) "past tense" to (^{44}) "any time"

a^{33}go^{22}ni^{23}sgv^{3}ʔi^2 one was target practicing (verb)
a^{33}go^{22}ni^{23}sgv^{44}ʔi^2 target (noun)

- The pronoun has not changed because it took the tone of the root.
- The rightmost long vowel increased from (^{23}) "past tense" to (^{44}) "any time"

$a^{21}hv^2sgo^{33}ʔi^2$ one sets it down (verb)
$nv^{22}wo^{32}ti^2$ $a^{44}hv^2sgi^2$ pharmacist (noun)

- Added the word $nv^{22}wo^{32}ti^2$ 'medicine' to describe what is being set down
- The rightmost long vowel increased from (^{22}) to (^{44}) "any time". Sometimes the rightmost long vowel is the pronoun itself.
- This derived noun means 'the one that sets down (on the counter) the medicine'.

$a^{21}tsi^{22}lv^{22}sgo^{33}ʔi^2$ one blooms (verb)
$a^{22}tsi^{22}lv^{44}sgi^2$ flower or bloomer (noun)

- The pronoun switches from (^{21}) "realistic" to (^{22}) "unrealistic.
- The rightmost long vowel increased from (^{23}) "past tense" to (^{44}) "any time"

Completive Stem Derivations

$u^{21}wv^{22}tsa^2hla^2nv^{23}ʔi^2$ one fried it (verb)
  $gv^{22}tsa^2hla^2nv^{44}ʔi^2$ fried (adjective)

- The verbal Set B pronoun ($u^{21}w$) switches to Set A (g).
- The rightmost long vowel increases from (^{23}) to (^{44}) tone.

Completive Conditional Derivation

$u^{22}da^{22}nv^0htv^2$ one's mind (noun)
$u^{22}da^{44}nv^0hti^2$ kind (adjective)
- The rightmost long vowel increased from (^{22}) to (^{44})

$u^{22}da^{22}nv^0hti^{23}sa^3hnv^{44}ʔi^2$ tamed or sober (adjective)
- The addition of the completive conditional suffix ($i^{23}sa^3hn$), meaning 'customarily' reflects that the root 'mind' is thoughtful in a social or customary way.
- The rightmost long vowel increased from (^{23}) "past tense" to (^{44}) "any time"

u^{21}de^{22}ho^{23}sv^{3}ʔi^2 one's embarrassed (verb)
u^{22}de^{22}ho^{23}sa^{3}ti^2 bashful (adjective)

- The pronoun switches from (^{21}) "realistic" to (^{22}) "unrealistic."
- The conditional suffix (a^{3}ti^2), meaning 'aptitude' is added to the completive stem of the verb.
- This is not a tonal derivation but it is a conjugated derivation where the use of this conditional suffix converts the word class to an adjective.

u^{21}lv^{33}nv^{23}ʔi^2 one put a flexible object in a container (verb)
di^{2}ga^{2}lv^{11}nv^{44}ʔi^2 noodles, pasta, or dumplings

- The pronoun switches from Set B (u$^{?1}$) to Set A (ga^2).
- The (^{33}) tone of the stem converts to (^{11}) marking derivational tone.
- The rightmost long vowel increases from (^{23}) to (^{44}) marking derivational word class change.

u^{21}wa^{33}tli^{22}sa^{2}hnv^{23}ʔi^2 one gathered it (verb)
ga^{33}tli^{22}sa^{2}hno^{3}hnv^{44}ʔi^2 totally (adverb)

- The pronoun switches from Set B (u^{21}w) to Set A (g).
- This is a completive verb stem with a completive conditional suffix (o^{3}hn), meaning 'as is customary'.
- The rightmost long vowel increases from (^{23}) to (^{44}).
- Simply by converting this completive word type to a Set A pronoun in the completive already conditions it for derivational meaning. It does this because Set B reflects a more personal experience while Set A reflects a general experience. This generality of the Set A pronoun is used widely throughout derivational processes.

ga^{2}ne^{23}la^2, one is living or residing (verb)

$a^2da^{22}ne^{23}lv^{44}ʔi^2$ a home or house (noun)

- Set A (g) switched to Set A (a) and the outsourced reflexive is added.

$u^{22}ne^{23}hla^3nv^{22}hi^2$ The Provider

- Set B pronoun
- The population suffix (ahn)
- The noun forming suffix (hi) meaning, 'with purpose'

$u^{22}ne^{23}hla^3nv^{44}hi^2$ a creator (of anything)

- The difference between this word and the previous is that addition of the rightmost long vowel tone is increased to a (^{44}) tone. This is "derivational tone" and that is why it isn't used on the word for 'The Provider' or 'God', because 'The Provider' is not viewed as coming from anything but rather everything comes from The Provider.

Infinitive Stem Derivations

$u^{22}dli^{11}sdi^2$ for one to pour (it) from a container (verb)
$a^3tli^{11}sdo^2hdi^2$ a liquid container (noun)

- Set B pronoun (u^{22}) switches to the Set A pronoun (a) with a tone change to (^{3}).
- The instrumental suffix (do^2hdi^2) is added to the infinitive stem to form a noun that is a tool for something or it is instrumental in doing something.

$u^{22}su^{23}hwi^3sdi^2$ for one to paint (verb)
$di^{22}su^{23}hwi^3sdi^2$ paint (noun)

- Essentially this derived noun is void of a pronoun and the unrealistic or deverbal pluralizer (di^{22}) is added directly to the stem to reflect that there is more than one paint and definitely more than one variety and also color.
- The use of the unrealistic pluralizer is what changes the word class of this verb to a noun.

u^{22}tsa^{2}yo^{22}sdi^2 for it to be poked (verb)
tsu^{22}tsa^{2}yo^{44}sdi^2 barbed or thorny (adjective)

- Here the pluralizer (ts) is used as is commonly used today however, much older written Cherokee would have shown this derivation written as di^2?u^{22}tsa^{2}yo^{44}sdi^2. This is merely showing change in pronunciation over time however, the older form reflects that morphological pattern of Cherokee much better.
- The rightmost long vowel increased from (^{22}) to (^{44}). Note: if it was said the old way instead of the (ts) pluralizer, the (^{44}) tone derivation would not have been necessary. The (di) prefix alone is enough to signal change in word class. By using the (ts) pluralizer, it looks too much like a verbal expression so the (^{44}) tone was used instead.

u^{21}lv^{23}gwo^{0}do^{2}hdi^2 for one to like it (verb)
u^{22}da^{0}lv^{44}gwo^{0}di^2 stuck up (adjective)
Lit. 'for one to like oneself'

- The pronoun switches from (^{21}) "realistic" to (^{22}) "unrealistic.
- The outsourced reflexive (adad) is added.
- The rightmost long vowel increased from (^{23}) to (^{44}) to reflect word class change.

u^{22}da^{11}dlo^{23}sdi^2 for one to put (it) around themselves (verb)
a^{2}da^{11}dlo^{23}sdi^2 belt (noun)

- Set B (u^{22}) switches to Set A (a) to signal a change from personal experience to shared experience. This change is all that is required to make a noun out of the infinitive stem.

u^{22}da^{22}ge^{22}hyu^{0}di^2 for one to love (verb)
a^{2}da^{22}ge^{22}hyu^{0}di^2 love (noun)

- Set B (u^{22}) switches to Set A (a) to signal a change from personal experience to shared experience. This change is all that is required to make a noun out of the infinitive stem.

$u^{22}da^{22}sda^{11}yv^{0}hdi^{23}ʔi$ for one to cook (verb)
$a^{2}da^{22}sda^{11}yv^{0}hdi^{44}yi^{2}$ kitchen (noun)
Lit. Place where one cooks

- Set B (u^{22}) switches to Set A (a^{2}) to signal a change from personal experience to shared experience.
- The rightmost long vowel increases from (^{23}) tone to (^{44}) tone to signal word class change.
- The suffix (yi) is added to show that this is a specific place that this action occurs at.

$u^{22}da^{2}wo^{11}sdi^{2}$ for one to bathe (verb)
$a^{2}da^{22}wo^{11}sdi^{44}yi^{2}$ bathtub or swimming pool
Lit. the place where one submerges themselves

- Set B (u^{22}) switches to Set A (a^{2}) to signal a change from personal experience to shared experience.
- The rightmost long vowel increases from (^{23}) tone to (^{44}) tone to signal word class change.
- The suffix (yi) is added to show that this is a specific place that this action occurs at.

Particle Derivation

$a^{2}da^{22}we^{33}hi^{2}$ magic or one's own magic or magician (noun)

[a]+[(a)da]+[we]+[hi]
[Set A]+[OS.REF]+[current or energy]+[purposeful suffix]

$a^{2}da^{22}we^{44}hi^{2}$ magical (adjective)

- The rightmost long vowel increased from (^{33}) to (^{44}) signaling a change in word class in order to describe something as being just like the noun.

na^{22}ni^{33}ʔa^2 the whole quantity or quality of them
[n(i)]+[ani]+[ʔ]+[a]
[summative]+[Set A. they]+[stationary]+[now]

i^{33}ya^{2}ni^{33}ʔi^2 the way or amount that they are
[iy]+[ani]+[ʔ]+[i]
[quantifier]+[SetA.they]+[stationary]+[to be]

gi^{23}ga^{3}ge^{44}ʔi^2 red (adjective)
       [giga]+[(i)geʔi]
       [blood]+[likeness]
- Adding the characterizer suffix (geʔi) creates the adjective by saying 'it is like blood'.

i^{22}ga^{33}dv^2 some (adjective)
       [iga]+[(i)dv]
       [amount]+[past participle suffix]
- It is common especially with particles for the literal morphological translation to not make perfect sense in English.

a^{0}sgo^{23}hi^{2}tsu^{0}gwi^0 one hundred (adjective)
[asgohi]+[ts(u)gwi]
[ten]+[lots]

tsu^{0}gwi^{44}sdi^2 a lot or many (adjective)
[ts(u)gwi]+[s]+[di]
[lots]+[subject focus]+[to be, infinitive suffix]

Verbs Derived From Verbs (Noun and Verb Incorporation)

u^{21}ne^{22}dli^{33}yv^{33}sv^{23}ʔi^{2} one changed it (verb)
u^{22}ne^{22}dli^{33}yv^{11}sdi^{2} for one to change it (verb)
a^{21}da^{2}ne^{22}dli^{33}yv^{11}sdi^{23}ha^{2} one is taking turns with another (verb)

- Set B (u^{22}) switched to Set A (a)
- The outsourced reflexive (adad) was added
- A new root suffix (h) was added to change the focus of the action.
- A new tense suffix (a) was added to convey that the action is happening right now.

[a]+[(a)da]+[nedliyvsdi]+[h]+[a]
[Set A]+[OS.REF]+[to change, infinitive stem root]+[motion focus]+[now]

a^{21}da^{2}**na^{32}**wa^{0}sdi^{23}ha^{2} one is taking off running
-a^{2}hyv^{23}s- nose (bound morpheme)
a^{21}hli^{2}yv^{23}sa^{3}**na^{11}**wa^{0}sdi^{23}ha^{2} one is snorting
[a]+[(a)li]+[(a)hyvs]+[anaw(a)sdi]+[h]+[a]
[SetA]+[S.REF]+[nose]+[being made to act]+[motion focus]+[now]
Lit. one's nose is being made to perform its duty

- When the infinitive stem is being used as a conditional suffix, the (^{32}) tone converts to the (^{11}) tone signaling word class change.

Writing To Reflect Tone

There are a total of eight tone articulators in the Syllabary. These articulators have been used by highly literate speakers for many years since the invention of the Syllabary. Their use as articulators can be seen throughout the Cherokee Phoenix Newspaper (before Removal) and this knowledge of the Syllabary seems to have been non-existent in the translation of the New Testament. The likely reason for this is because the New Testament was translated either in whole or in large part by a non-Native speaker.

The eight articulatory Syllabary characters are shown below. These are the characters that are used to convey tone change. Additionally, there are two sets that are used to convey how familiar with the object the subject is. The characters that alternate to show familiarity are θ/G and Ꭽ/Ꮭ. This is useful to the recipient of a written letter because it lets the reader know how much the writer may know about a particular subject. It also does not matter which character in the word substitutes for an articulator because when we see that an articulator is being used, we know immediately that the rightmost long vowel will need to be read with a higher tone.

Tone Articulators: Ꮎ(ka), G(nah), Ꮝ(s), Ꮤ(ta), Ꮦ(te), Ꮨ(ti), Ꮬ(dla), Ꮏ(hna)
Familiarity Alternates: θ(na) Ꮭ(tla)

Each of the above articulators alternate with their non aspirant forms to reflect words that have tone change or have changed word class tonally.

E.g. ga alternates with ka
na alternates with nah
s has no alternate (E.g. this is why Sequoyah wrote his name as ᏍᏇᏬᎤᏋ.
He used the (Ꮝ) character to indicate that his name is a
proper noun.)
da alternates with ta
de alternate with te

di alternates with ti
dla alternates with tla

a^{21}dle^{33}sgv^{23}ʔi^{2} ᎠᏞᏍᎬᎢ one was turning off (verb)
a^{22}dle^{33}sgv^{44}hi^{2} ᎠᏞᏍᎬᎯ a turn off (noun)

a^{21}do^{33}ni^{22}sgv^{23}ʔi^{2} ᎠᏙᏂᏍᎬᎢ one was talking to themselves (verb)
a^{22}do^{33}ni^{44}sgi^{2} ᎠᏙᏂᏍᎩ sorcerer
The agentive suffix [sgi] already signals a tone change therefore, an articulator is not necessary.

a^{21}de^{33}yo^{2}hv^{23}ʔi^{2} ᎠᏕᏲᎲᎢ one was going around a curve (verb)
a^{22}de^{33}yo^{2}hv^{44}hi^{2} ᎠᏕᏲᎲᎯ a curve (noun)

a^{33}go^{22}ni^{23}sgv^{3}ʔi^{2} ᎠᎪᏂᏍᎬᎢ one was target practicing (verb)
a^{33}go^{22}ni^{23}sgv^{44}hi^{2} ᎠᎪᏂᏍᎬᎯ target (noun)

a^{21}hv^{2}sgo^{33}ʔi^{2} ᎠᎲᏍᎪᎢ one sets it down (verb)
a^{44}hv^{2}sgi^{2} ᎠᎲᏍᎩ a setter downer (noun)

a^{21}tsi^{22}lv^{22}sgo^{33}ʔi^{2} ᎠᏥᎸᏍᎪᎢ one blooms (verb)
a^{22}tsi^{22}lv^{44}sgi^{2} ᎠᏥᎸᏍᎩ flower or bloomer (noun)

u^{21}wv^{22}tsa^{2}hla^{2}nv^{23}ʔi^{2} ᎤᏮᏣᏝᏅᎢ one fried it (verb)
gv^{22}tsa^{2}hla^{2}nv^{44}hi^{2} ᎬᏣᏝᏅᎯ fried (adjective)

u^{22}da^{22}nv^{0}htv^{2} ᎤᏓᏅᏛ one's mind (noun)
u^{22}da^{44}nv^{0}hti^{2} ᎤᏓᏅᏘ kind (adjective)

u^{21}de^{22}ho^{23}sv^{3}ʔi^{2} ᎤᏕᎰᏍᏒᎢ one embarrassed (verb)
u^{22}de^{22}ho^{23}sa^{3}ti^{2} ᎤᏕᎰᏍᏌᏘ bashful (adjective)

u^{21}lv^{33}nv^{23}ʔi^{2} ᎤᎸᏅᎢ one put a flexible object in a container (verb)
di^{2}ga^{2}lv^{11}nv^{44}hi^{2} ᏗᎦᎸᏅᎯ noodles, pasta, or dumplings (noun)

u^{21}wa^{33}tli^{22}sa^{2}hnv^{23}ʔi^{2} ᎤᏩᏟᏍᏌᏅᎢ one gathered it (verb)
ga^{33}tli^{22}sa^{2}hno^{3}hnv^{44}hi^{2} ᎦᏟᏌᏃᏅᎯ totally (adverb)
u^{22}ne^{23}hla^{3}nv^{22}hi^{2} ᎤᏁᎳᏅᎯ The Provider (God)
u^{22}ne^{23}tla^{3}nv^{44}hi^{2} ᎤᏁᏝᏅᎯ a creator (of anything)

u²²dli¹¹sdi² OᵒCꙷꙷↃ for one to pour (it) from a container (verb)
a³tli¹¹sdo²hdi² ꓓCꙷↅↃ a liquid container (noun)

u²²su²³hwi³sdi² OᵒꙷↀↂꙷꙷↃ for one to pain or color (verb)
di²²su²³hwi³sdi² ↃꙷↀↂꙷꙷↃ paint (noun)

u²²tsa²yo²²sdi² OᵒGↄꙷↃ for it to be poked (verb)
tsu²²tsa²yo⁴⁴sti² ↈGↄꙷↄ barbed or thorny (adjective)

u²¹lv²³gwo⁰do²hdi² OᵒꓕↂꙷↅↃ for one to like it (verb)
u²¹da⁰lv⁴⁴gwo⁰ti² Oᵒↈꓕↂꙷↄ stuck up (adjective)

u²²da¹¹dlo²³sdi² OᵒↈꙷↀↃ for one to put (it) around themselves (verb)
a²da¹¹dlo²³sdi² ꓓↈꙷↀↃ a belt (noun)

u²²da²²ge²²yu⁰hdi² OᵒↈⱤGꙷↃ for one to love (verb)
a²da²²ge²²yu⁰hdi² ꓓↈⱤGꙷↃ love (noun)

u²²da²²sda¹¹yv⁰hdi²³ʔi² OᵒↈꙷↈBↃT for one to cook (verb)
a²da²²sda¹¹yv⁰hdi⁴⁴yi² ꓓↈꙷↈBↃↄ kitchen (noun)

u²²da²wo¹¹sdi² OᵒↈↄꙷↃ for one to bathe (verb)
a²da²²wo¹¹sdi⁴⁴yi² ꓓↈↄꙷↃↄ bathtub or swimming pool

a²da²²we³³hi²hi² ꓓↈↄↄↃↃ magic or magician (noun)
a²da²we⁴⁴hi²³yu³ ꓓↈↄↃGↂ magical (adjective)

na²²ni³³ʔa² ↂhꓓ the whole quantity or quality of them

Note: articulators are not necessary for particles unless their formation required a tone change. E.g. tsu⁰gwi⁴⁴sdi⁰ would be written tsu⁰gwi⁴⁴sti² ↈↀↂꙷↃ. In such a case, an articulator would have to be used to show that the rightmost long vowel will have a higher tone. Particles are combinations of bound morphemes that have set tone and that is why we don't need an articulator to know how they should be pronounced.

i³³ya²ni³³ʔi² TⱭhT the way or amount that they are

gi²³ga³ge⁴⁴ʔi² ᏤᏚᏐᎢ red (adjective)

i²²ga³³dv² TᏚᎶ° some (adjective)

a⁰sgo²³hi²tsu⁰gwi² DⱭAᎫᏦ° one hundred (adjective)

tsu⁰gwi⁴⁴sti² ᏍᎶⱭᎫ a lot or many

Expressing Familiarity

na²²sgi² ΘⱭᎩ he/she/it "not familiar to the subject"
       nah²²sgi² GⱭᎩ he/she/it "familiar to the subject"

na²²hna³ ΘᏖ that place "unfamiliar to the subject"
       nah²²hna³ GᏖ that place "familiar to the subject"

di²²gwa²da²²ti²nah²ʔv⁴⁴hi² ᏗᏓᏖᏗGiᎫ My family "they are familiar"
nah= familiarity
hi= rightmost long vowel tone change

du²²da²²ti²hna?v⁴⁴hi² SᏦᎫ<u>t</u>iᎫ his/her family "not familiar"
hna= not familiar
hi= rightmost long vowel tone change

7.0 MORPHOLOGY & TONE

Throughout the Cherokee-English Dictionary (CED) Durbin Feeling—1975, you will find multiple (what I call) "tone contractions". These contractions are no different than "are not" and "aren't", in English. These are simply contractions that we are able to create in Cherokee because our language is tonal. It is also important to note that these contractions are not grammatical or based on any rule in our language. They occurred the same way English contractions occurred—people just started saying them and they became accepted amongst speaking groups, communities, and entire regions.

Documenting these types of contractions without explanation however, make it extremely difficult for someone to learn the correct morphemes, and makes it almost impossible to build a Root Word Method teaching curriculum. In this section, I will show you several examples of documented verbs that contain tone contractions, and I will also give you the decontracted form of those verbs. It may interest you to know, that the decontracted forms cause the pronunciation to be much more tonal and reflects the speaking patterns of the Elders in my family that I grew up around in the Sequoyah county area.

It is also important to note that, Cherokee has a tonal feature that is well documented in the Iroquoian language family—that feature is known as "penultimate syllable stress". This means that the right-most long vowel has tone stress by default. Many Elder speakers still to this day pronounce penultimate syllable stress however, most speakers today prodominately contract penultimate syllable stress (as shown below), which dillutes a large part of our languages' musical quality.

one sees another or it

Contracted Form:	$a^{21}go^{22}hwa^{0}ti^{3}ha^{2}$
Decontracted Form:	$a^{21}go^{22}hwa^{0}hti^{23}ha^{2}$

one is cutting it

Contracted Form:	$a^{21}gv^{22}ha^{2}li^{3}ha^{2}$
Decontracted Form:	$a^{21}gv^{22}ha^{2}li^{23}ha^{2}$

one is smothering or suffocating another

Contracted Form:	$a^{21}ha^{2}wo^{33}sdi^{2}ha^{2}$
Decontracted Form:	$a^{21}ha^{2}wo^{33}sdi^{23}ha^{2}$

one wants it

    Contracted Form: $u^{21}du^{22}li^{3}ha^{2}$

    Decontracted Form: $a^{21}du^{22}li^{23}ha^{2}$

one is bouncing it

    Contracted Form: $a^{21}da^{2}di^{23}nv^{32}\mathbf{di^{2}}ha^{2}$

    Decontracted Form: $a^{21}da^{2}di^{23}nv^{32}\mathbf{di^{23}}ha^{2}$

one is praying

    Contracted Form: $a^{21}da^{22}do^{23}li^{32}s\mathbf{di^{2}}ha^{2}$

    Decontracted Form: $a^{21}da^{22}do^{23}li^{32}s\mathbf{di^{23}}ha^{2}$

one is committing adultery

    Contracted Form: $a^{21}da^{22}hyo^{33}\underline{ne^{2}ha}^{2}$

    Decontracted Form: $a^{21}da^{22}hyo^{33}\underline{ne^{23}ha}^{2}$

       The underlined portion above is the "applicative conditional suffix" and morphologically has a long vowel. Due to the fact that the applicative suffix happens to be in the penultinate syllable—choosing to contract the tone on a word such as this makes it difficult for students, linguists, etc., to be able to detect morpheme boundaries or recognize the meaning of the word.

       Tone contraction is a natural part of Cherokee communication, but ideally it is my belief that students need access to complete morphemes in order to grasp the language, and once able to communicate can begin to contract the same as fluent speakers. A strong foundation of Cherokee thought must first be formed and then ACCURATE shortcuts can grow from those skills.

8.0 PRONOUN TONE (EXPRESSING RELATION & REALITY)

THE FOUR STEMS	REALITY
Incompletive Stem	REAL/UNREAL
Completive Stem	REAL/UNREAL
Immediate Stem	REAL/UNREAL
Infinitive Stem	UNREAL

Incompletive (REAL)

ᎾᏂᏪᏍᎬᎢ	na^{21}ni^{22}we^{11}sgv^{23}ʔi^2	She was stating.
ᎦᏬᏂᏍᎬᎢ	ga^{2}wo^{33}ni^{22}sgv^{23}ʔi^2	She was speaking.

Incompletive (UNREAL)

ᎦᏬᏂᏍᎨᎢ	ga^{2}wo^{33}ni^{22}sge^{33}ʔi^2	She was speaking (supposedly)
ᎠᏂᏬᏂᏍᎨᏍᏗ	a^{22}ni^{22}wo^{33}ni^{22}sge^{33}sdi^2	They will speak.
ᎠᏗᏔᏍᎪᎢ	a^{22}di^{22}ta^{2}sgo^{33}ʔi^2	She usually drinks.

Completive (REAL)

ᎤᏬᏂᏒᎢ	u^{21}wo^{33}ni^{22}sv^{23}ʔi^2	She spoke.
ᎤᏃᏕᏨᎢ	u^{21}hne^{33}tsv^{23}ʔi^2	She stated.

Completive (UNREAL)

ᎤᏬᏂᏎᎢ	u^{22}wo^{33}ni^{22}se^{33}ʔi^2	She spoke (supposedly)
ᎭᏥᏃᏥ	da^{2}tsi^{2}hne^{33}tsi^2	I will state.
ᎯᏃᏕᏨᎢ	hi^{2}hne^{33}tsv^{22}ʔi^2	Speak later.
ᏛᏂᏬᏂᏏ	dv^{22}ni^{22}wo^{33}ni^{22}si^2	They will speak.

Immediate (REAL)

| ᎠᏂᎩ | hi²hne²²gi² | (Immediate Past) | You just stated it. |
| ᏥᎣᏇᎷᏔ | cha²di²²ta² | (Immediate Past) | You just drank it. |

Immediate (UNREAL)

| ᎠᏂᎩ | hi²hne¹¹gi² | (Command) | State it! |
| ᎣᏇᎷᏔ | ha²di²³ta² | (Command) | Drink it! |

Infinitive (UNREAL)

ᎤᏂᎢᏙᎵ	u²²hne²ʔi⁰sdi²	For him/her to state.
ᎤᏬᎯᎠᏙᎵ	u²²wo¹¹ni²³hi³sdi²	For him/her to speak.
ᎤᎷᏔᏙᎵ	u²²di²²ta²sdi²	For him/her to drink it.

STEM OVERVIEW

Incompletive Stem	Action was, is, or will be happening.
Completive Stem	Action did or will happen.
Immediate Stem	Make action happen!/Action just now happened.
Infinitive Stem	For the action to happen (abstract idea)

8.1 OTHER REALITY DISTINGUISHING FEATURES

[h] & [ʔ] Alternation, [h] deletion, Pronoun Tone Shift

Glottal = 1st Person Reality   [h] = 3rd Person (Does not affect 1st Person)

Example: $ga^2de^{22}lo^2\underline{ʔo}^{22}sga^2$ Concerns my directly

     $a^{21}de^{22}lo^2\underline{ho}^{22}sga^2$ Does not affect me

[h] Deletion = 1st Person Reality   [h] = 3rd Person (Does not affect 1st Person)

Example: $ga^2de^{22}\_lo^2hgwa^3ʔa^2$ Concerns me directly

     $a^{21}de^{22}\underline{hl}o^2hgwa^3ʔa^2$ Does not affect me

tsi^{21} = 1st Person Reality ka^2 = 3rd Person (Does not affect 1st Person)

Example: $tsi^{\underline{21}}ne^{33}ga^2$ *I'm stating.* Concerns me directly

     $ka^{\underline{2}}ne^{33}ga^2$ *She is stating.* Doesn't affect me

This feature is necessary to maintain and respect the individuality of each person and also to foster self-awareness of what truly affects us in life. This shows that our people have a built in understanding of how to cope with the positives and negatives of life. By constantly focusing on what is real and unreal, we are able to let go of many problems that we can sometimes treat as "real" in English, but do not exist in the realm of reality in traditional Cherokee thought.

ATONIC AND TONIC PRONOUNS

The terms atonic and tonic refer to how the tones are perceived and articulated in predictable areas within the language. It is important to realize that these are not grammatical features but reflections of Spiritual belief imbedded within the language itself. Atonic refers to when the pronoun (in this case) takes an atonic form i.e. reflecting that the idea of the conjugated verb is in an unrealistic state. Unrealistic states are reflected in the language not only by pronouns but also by pre-pronoun prefixes, stem, and suffixes. Whenever you say an action 'could happen', 'supposedly happened', 'is in command form', or is an abstract notion like 'the infinitive', you will need to convert the pronoun to its atonic form. In contract, when the action is 'truly' a part of reality and actually 'was' or 'is' happening—you will need to use the tonic form of the pronoun. Simply by arming you with the traditional knowledge of why we shift the tone, you are able to apply the knowledge in a traditional way.

Atonic and tonic shift of the pronoun occurs on all pronoun forms unless their default tone is already comprised of (2) tones. In the event this happens you don't need to change anything and can simply say it the same way whether the action is real or unrealistic. The conditional suffixes and prefixes in this case are enough to convey this understanding.

a^{21}	REAL
a^{22}	UNREAL
$a^{21}gw$	REAL
$a^{22}gw$	UNREAL
u^{21}	REAL
u^{22}	UNREAL
$a^{21}ni^{22}$	REAL
$a^{22}ni^{22}$	UNREAL
$u^{21}ni^{22}$	REAL
$u^{22}ni^{22}$	UNREAL

9.0 WHAT IS POLYSYNTHESIS?

1)   Polypersonal Agreement
2)   Noun Incorporation
3)   Extensive Use of Suffixes
4)   Relatively Free Word Order
5)   Predominately Head-Marking

General Remarks...

Prefixes and suffixes together are called 'affixes'. These convey information that other languages need seperate words to express.

Affixes identify subject or with intransitives the object, tense, aspect, and mood distinctions, noun roots Incorporated or compounded with the verb, direction and adverbial notions, etc.

Everything centers around the root word. Most of these highly inflected (fully conjugated) root words are fully complete sentences with regards to what constitutes complete sentences in other languages such as, English.

Polypersonal Agreement

This means both the subject and the object are marked on the root word.

    E.g., $\underline{a^{21}tsi^{22}lv^{23}gwo^{32}di^2(?a)}$
              'He/She likes him/her'

Not all languages have fused personal affixes. Iroquoian language do however.
E.g.   In Seneca;

        she = 2P subj. & PL obj.

        ēshéo:wí
        (FUT + 2P subj/PL obj. + tell + punctual)

        'You will tell them.'   *This is a "one-word" complete sentence.*

Noun Incorporation

This allows us to alter known concepts giving them a more specific meaning.

In English: blackberry + picking = blackberry-picking

The above formula for noun incorporation is:

[Root Stem + Verb = New (Specific) Verb]

These compound expressions are made to express very specific actions rather than general ones.

**Shared Characteristics of Languages
With Noun Incorpoation**

Valency Reducing (by one)

- Transitive > Instransitive
- Ditransitive > Transitive

Incorporated Nouns are Uninflected

- No case marking
- No plural marking
- No noun class
- No articles
- No demonstratives

Agents are Never Incorporated

- No beneficiaries or receivers

Noun-Incorporation is Dead? What??

It has been said by other linguists (Mithun primarily, and the other quote her) that noun-incorporation is archaic and not a functional part of contemporary Cherokee. This statement is based on (a handful) of forms analyzed and in my professional opinion—these are not enough forms or substantial evidence to make such a claim. I have personally incorporated nouns and witnessed them incorporated in my lifetime and—I or any of the Elder speakers I have spoken with—are by no means "archaic". To prove that this process is alive and well, we will translate the above English example of noun-incorporation, "blackberry-picking".

> Step 1: We must isolate the noun-stem. The noun we will be incorporating is
> "blackberry".
>
> $$ka^2nu^{22}ga^3?lv^4$$

> Step 2: We now have to isolate the verb we want to incorporate with the
> noun. We have to use the infinitve tense form of "picking" without
> any prefix inflection.
>
> E.g. $u^2wu^{22}te^{11}sdi^2 >$ $u^{22}te^{11}sdi^2$

> Step 3: We now have to convert the root-stem of the verb back to its tonic or
> tonal form.
>
> E.g. $u^{22}te^{11}sdi^2$ $>$ $u^{22}te^{33}sdi^2$

> Step 4: We now convert the noun "blackberry" to its stem form.
>
> E.g. $ka^2nu^{22}ga^3?lv^4 >$ $hnu^{22}ga^3?l$

> Step 5: Now we follow the rule for noun-incorporation!
> Rule: The incorporated noun-stem is preposed (connected before) to the
> verb. A connector vowel /a/ is inserted between them if the noun-stem ends in a consonant and the verb root begins in a consonant.
>
> Let's look at both of words in the order in which they are supposed to
> connect. If the noun-stem is preposed to the verb—that means the
> first word we need is "blackberry" followed by the verb "picking".

E.g. $hnu^{22}ga^3?l$ "blackberry" $u^{22}de^{33}sdi^2$ "removing
                                                          it from hanging"

We can see that the noun-stem has NO vowel and the joining verb-stem begins with a vowel. Therefore, we can just connect the two terms because CVC phonological rules are being followed.

Thus, we end up with: -hnu^{22}ga^{3}ʔlu^{22}de^{33}sdi^2-

This is our complete "incorporated noun" root that we can further conjugate.

Step 6: We now rely on what we have learned about pronoun prefixes so we can classify this correctly. All we know is the following:

Our root: -hnu^{22}ga^{3}ʔlu^{22}de^{33}sdi^2-

Intended Person: 3P Singular

Intended Time Frame: Incompletive Past (i.e. was doing "verb")

To determing whether we use Set A (shared-experience) or Set B (individual experience), we look at the noun-root "blackberry". This noun was originally ka^{2}nu^{22}ga^{3}ʔlv^4, and   [ka] is the Set A, 3P pronoun [ga]. The aspirated form [ka] comes from the /h/ of the root. Knowing that [ka] comes from an /h/ in the root helps you to realize what the root should be in isolation. This also tells us that this verb is classified as Set A by default so the conjugation follows the rules of default Set A conjugation.

Set A Default Conjugation Rules:

Present Stem	Set A pronoun
Incompletive Stem	Set A pronoun
Completive Stem	Set B pronoun
Immediate Stem	Set A pronoun
Infinitive Stem	Set B pronoun

Step 7: We can now conjugate the stem forms for 3P singular subject and plural object—because why would anyone just pick one blackberry?? Also, this allows us to see what happens to the stems with regards to additional particles to make the incorporated noun work grammatically.

Conjugated Forms

Present   da^{21}hnu^{22}ga^{3}ʔlu^{22}de^{33}sdi^{2}ha^{2} /h/ motion focus
           'He/She is blackberry-picking'

Habitual   da^{21}hnu^{2}ga^{3}ʔlu^{22}de^{33}sdi^{22}sgo^{33}ʔi^{2} /i^{22}/ continuation
                                                                /sg/ subj./obj. focus
           'He/She is usually blackberry-picking'

Completive du^{21}hnu^{23}ga^{3}ʔlu^{22}de^{33}sta^{2}nv^{23}ʔi^{2} /a<hn/ purposive (intent)
           'He/She had been blackberry-picking'

Imperative ta^{2}hnu^{22}ga^{2}ʔlu^{22}de^{11}sda^{2} /e^{11}sda^{2}/ atonic imperative
           'You be blackberry-picking!'

Infinitive tsu^{22}hnu^{22}ga^{2}ʔlu^{22}de^{11}sdo^{2}hdi^{2} /o^{2}hdi^{2}/ instrumental infix
           'For him/her to be blackberry-picking'

10.0 WHEN CLAUSES

WHAT YOU NEED TO ASK YOURSELF:

1) Is the statement real or hypothetical?
   The answer to this will tell you which pre-pronoun prefixes, pronouns, and suffixes you need to use.

2) When is the action of the verb occuring?
   This answer will tell you which stem you will need to use.
   E.g. either incompletive stem, completive stem, immediate stem, or the infinitive stem.

What does she usually do on the weekend?
do^{22}hnv^{3} u^{44}sdi^{2} a^{11}dv^{33}ne^{2}ho^{33}? sv^{22}na^{0}do^{23}da^{2}gwa^{11}sdi^{2} _____?

Finished: u^{22}sgwa^{3}hdv^{44}ʔi^{2}

I guess we will let the dog outside when that happens.
a^{22}se^{33}di^{32} yi^{22}da^{2}li^{22}sgo^{22}lv^{0}da^{11}si^{0} u^{22}nv^{22}go^{22}ʔi^{2}sdi^{23}ʔi^{2} sgi^{2} _____.

It had gone on: nu^{22}li^{0}sta^{2}ni^{23}do^{32}lv^{44}ʔi^{2}

I was about to eat when my son started crying.
da^{2}ga^{2}li^{11}sda^{32}yv^{22}ni^{33}sv^{2} a^{22}gwe^{23}tsi^{2} a^{2}tsu^{23}tsa^{2} _____ a^{21}dlo^{22}hyi^{3}hv^{23}ʔi^{2}

Begun: u^{21}le^{22}nv^{22}hv^{44}ʔi^{2}

She is getting better at speaking Cherokee.
da^{22}tse^{33}la^{32}ga^{2}dv^{33} tsa^{2}la^{2}gi^{0} _____

He or She was speaking: ga^{2}wo^{33}ni^{22}sgv^{44}ʔi^{2}

I want to be a firefighter when I grow up.
di²²gv⁰dla²di¹¹sgi⁴ ya²²gwa²li⁰sdo³hdi² a²¹gwa²du²²li³ho³ _____

I grew: a²¹gwa²tv²sv⁴⁴ʔi²

My stomach hurt when I ate.
a²²gi⁰sgwo⁴⁴hli⁰ tsa²¹gwe²³i⁰sda¹¹ne²²lv² _____

I finished eating: a²¹gwa²li⁰sda³²yv⁰hno³hnv⁴⁴ʔi²

O°ℰꙅS.Ꝏ DꙆԺꙄꙨꙆ O°ꙆꙌꙠPT ꙆSSꙆ O°ꙶꙶθ.
U²wo²²du⁴⁴hi² a²da¹¹dlo²³sdi⁰ u²¹da³³dlo²²hlv²³ʔi² di²ga²²du³³hv⁴ u²we⁴⁴na².
She put on a pretty belt when she went to town.
       Went. u²¹we⁰⁰nv³³sv²³ʔi²

RWꙆ ꙨꙆθ ꙨꙆꙆꙨꙆ O°ꙆꙆꙠ-RT.
E²²la²di² wu²¹di⁴⁴na² sgwa²²hle⁴⁴sdi⁰ u²¹da²di²³nv³²sv²³ʔi².
When he threw the ball down, it bounced.
       Threw it there: wu²¹di²³nv³²sv²³ʔi²

O°ꙨꙆꙆ AꙶꙄ SAꙶꙄꙨE, O°ꙆꙨꙨWO-T.
u⁴⁴sgwa³hda² go²¹hwe²³li³²sgv², u²¹da²²hya³²sta²nv²³ʔi².
When he finished writing, he stretched.
       Finished: u²¹sgwa³hdv²³ʔi²

O°ꙄꙨꙆBꙆ GꙶCTGꙆ, Ꙇ ꙆꙅꙆGꙶ ꙨꙆꙶꙨꙆꙨꙆAT .
u²²li⁰sda¹¹yv⁰hdi² yu²¹hli²²ʔi³lo⁴⁴hla² tla³ hi²lv²³hi³yu⁴ ya²²le²²hwi²sdi²³sgo³ʔi².
When it's time for him to eat, he never stops.
       Came time: u²¹hli²²ʔi³lo³²hlv²³ʔi²

YC ꙆꙨꙆꙶꙨE O°ꙀꙶSθ, O°ꙆꙀꙆꙨWO-T.
gi²²hli⁰ da²¹si²hwi³sgv² u²¹tv²³ga⁴⁴na², u²¹da²na³²wa⁰sta²nv²³ʔi².
When he heard the dog bark, he ran.
       Heard: u²¹tv²³ga³²nv²³ʔi²

ᎠᎹᏟᎬᎾᎨ ᎤᎧᏏᏪᏫᏳᏗᏫ ᎤᎧᏏᏨᏒᎢ.
a²ge²²hyu²³tsa⁰ u²¹ga⁰ta³²sda¹¹ne⁴⁴la² u²¹de²²ho²³sv³ʔi².
When the girl winked at him, he got embarrassed.
      Winked at another: u²¹ga⁰ta³²sda¹¹ne²²lv²³ʔi²

ᎠᏣᏍᏗᎧᏗ ᎠᎩᎦᏩᏍᏗ ᏍᏍᏏᏯᏗD.
a²²gwa²de²²tv⁰hdi² a²¹gi²lv²³gwo⁰di⁰ yi²ga²da²wo⁴⁴ʔa².
I like to dive when I'm swimming.
      He or She is swimming: a²¹da²wo³³ʔa²

ᎠᏩ ᏍᏋᏏᏩᎦ ᎠᏍᎾᏫᏍᎠᎢ.
Gogi yi²nu⁴⁴li⁰sta²na² a²¹ga²²na²wo²²sgo³³ʔi².
When it becomes summer, it gets warm.
      Happened: nu²¹li⁰sta²nv²³ʔi²

ᎦᎳᏫ ᏋᏏᏩᎦ ᎤᎧᏫᏩ, ᎤᎧᏣᏫᎢᏒᎢ.
Ga²²da²³ha⁴ nu⁴⁴li⁰sta²na² u²²hna²wo³, u²¹hna²wa³³ʔi²²yv³³sv²³ʔi².
When his shirt got dirty, he changed it.
      Happened: nu²¹li⁰sta²nv²³ʔi²

     This clause could also be made by adding the four tone to the regular
     past tense stem form. E.g., nu⁴⁴li⁰sta²nv²—because this action actually,
     truly took place.

ᎠᏫᏩᏗ ᏪᎬᏩᏍᏪᏑᏫ, ᎠᏗᏫᏗᎧ ᎠᏣᏨᏩᎢ.
Go²²hu⁴⁴sdi² ya²²gv²²sga²hla³²ne⁴⁴la², a²hi⁴⁴di⁰ a²¹hwa²hti²³sgo³ʔi².
When something is hidden from him, he finds it easily.
    It was hidden from him or her: a²¹gv²²sga²hla³²ne²²lv²³ʔi²

When the Sun was shining...
ᎾᎥᏏᏍ ᎤᎧᏟᏩᏙ
nv²²do²²gv²³yi⁴ a²¹ga³³li⁴⁴sgv²
      It was shining: a²¹ga³³li²²sgv²³ʔi²

When the Sun shines...

nv^{22}do^{22}gv^{23}yi^{4} yu^{22}ga^{33}li^{44}sa^{2}

Shined: u^{21}ga^{33}li^{22}sv^{23}ʔi^{2}

The Sun just warmed me when it shined just now.

nv^{22}do^{22}gv^{23}yi^{4} a^{21}gi^{2}ga^{22}na^{2}wo^{22}sda^{32}si^{0} tsa^{21}ga^{11}li^{23}hi^{2}

It just now shined: wa^{21}ga^{22}li^{23}hi^{2}

11.0 NEW TERMS—TRADITIONAL METHOD

New Vocabulary:

ᏗᎦᏛ̃ᏍᎤᎵᏃᎵ di^{22}ka^{2}hyu^{3}hga^{2}nv^{22}li^{23}ye^{32}di^2

ᏗᎦᏛ̃ᎩᎶᏍᏗ di^{22}ka^{2}hyu^{3}hgi^{22}lo^{33}sdi^0

ᏗᏣᎵᎥᏐᎯᏗ di^{22}ga^{2}hlv^{22}gi^{33}sdo^{2}hdi^2

Familiar Word/Revived Verb: watching

a^{23}ya^{32}wi^{0}sga^2 she or he is watching
tsi^{23}ya^{32}wi^{0}sga^2 I'm watching
a^{23}ya^{32}wi^{0}sgo^{33}ʔi^2 she or he usually watches
a^{23}ya^{32}sgv^{23}ʔi^2 she or he was watching
u^{21}wa^{23}ya^{32}wi^{0}sv^{23}ʔi^2 she or he watched
u^{22}wa^{23}ya^{32}wi^{0}sdi^2 for her or him to watch

yu^{22}wa^{23}ya^{32}wi^{0}se^{33}ʔi^2 she or he would have watched
a^{22}ni^{23}ya^{32}wi^{0}sgi^4 guards or soldiers
u^{22}ni^{23}ya^{32}wi^{0}sv^{44}hi^2 the guard (a specific guard)

E.g.   sv^{22}no^{23}yi^0 u^{22}ni^{23}ya^{32}wi^{0}sv^{44}hi^2 The Night Watch

i^{22}tsa^{2}da^{23}ya^{32}wi^{0}sge^{33}sdi^{2}wu^{3}di^{44}na^2 You all be on guard.

New Verb: snapping fingers

de^{33}ga^{2}ye^{22}sa^{2}no^{22}hyv^{22}hli^{2}sdi^{3}ha^2 she is snapping her fingers

de^{33}tsi^{2}ye^{22}sa^{2}no^{22}yv^{11}li^{2}sdi^{3}ha^2 I'm snapping my fingers

du^{21}ye^{22}sa^{2}no^{22}hyv^{22}hli^{2}sta^{3}nv^{23}ʔi^2 she snapped her fingers

de^{33}ga^{2}ye^{22}sa^{2}no^{22}hyv^{22}hli^{2}sdi^{23}sgo^{3}ʔi^2 he or she snaps his or her fingers

ti^{22}ye^{22}sa^{2}no^{22}hyv^{22}hli^{2}sda^2 snap your fingers

de^{33}ʔu^{22}ye^{22}sa^{2}no^{22}hyv^{22}hli^{2}sdo^{3}hdi^2 for her to snap her fingers

Verb: Crossing Arms

de^{33}ga^{2}do^{22}ya^{2}hne^{33}sga^{2}li^{23}ha^{2}	he or she is crossing his or her arms
de^{33}tsi^{2}do^{22}ya^{2}hne^{33}sga^{2}li^{23}ha^{2}	I'm crossing my arms
du^{21}do^{22}ya^{2}hne^{33}sga^{2}lv^{22}hv^{23}ʔi^{2}	he or she crossed his or her arms
de^{33}ga^{2}do^{22}ya^{2}hne^{33}sga^{2}li^{23}sgo^{3}ʔi^{2}	he or she crosses his or her arms
ti^{22}do^{22}ya^{2}hne^{33}sga^{2}la^{2}	cross your arms
de^{33}ʔu^{22}do^{22}ya^{2}hne^{11}sga^{3}hlv^{0}hdi^{2}	for him or her to cross his or her arms

Verb: Crossing Legs

de^{33}ga^{2}la^{11}ya^{2}hne^{33}sga^{2}li^{33}ha	he or she is crossing his or her legs
de^{33}tsi^{2}la^{11}ya^{2}hne^{33}sga^{2}li^{33}ha^{2}	I'm crossing my legs
du^{21}la^{11}ya^{2}hne^{33}sga^{2}lv^{22}hv^{23}ʔi^{2}	he or she crossed his or her arms
de^{33}ga^{2}la^{11}ya^{2}hne^{33}sga^{2}li^{23}sgo^{3}ʔi^{2}	he or she crosses his or her arms
ti^{22}la^{11}ya^{2}hne^{33}sga^{2}la^{2}	cross your legs
de^{33}ʔu^{22}la^{11}ya^{2}hne^{11}sga^{3}hlv^{0}hdi^{2}	for him or her to cross his or her legs

Verb: Giving a High Five

u^{21}do^{22}ya^{2}lv^{33}ni^{2}ha^2	he or she is high fiving him or her
tsi^{22}ya^{2}do^{22}ya^{2}lv^{33}ni^{2}ha^2	I'm high fiving him or her
u^{21}do^{22}ya^{2}lv^{23}ni^{32}lv^{23}ʔi^2	he or she high fived him or her
hi^{22}ya^{2}do^{22}ya^{2}lv^{22}ni^{11}ga^2	give him or her a high five
u^{22}do^{22}ya^{2}lv^{23}ni^{32}sdi^2	for him or her to give him or her a high five
sgwa^{2}do^{22}ya^{2}lv^{22}ni^{11}ga^2	give me a high five

Verb: Flipping Someone Off
(literally to stand a finger up at another)

a^{21}li^{0}ye^{22}sa^{2}le^{2}hda^{32}ne^{22}ha^2	he or she is flipping him or her off
tsi^{22}ya^{2}li^{11}sa^{2}le^{2}hda^{32}ne^{22}ha^2	I'm flipping him or her off
u^{21}li^{0}ye^{22}sa^{2}le^{2}hda^{32}ne^{22}lv^{23}ʔi^2	he or she flipped him or her off
a^{21}li^{0}ye^{22}sa^{2}le^{2}hda^{32}ne^{22}ho^{33}ʔi^2	he or she flips him or her off
hi^{22}ya^{2}li^{11}ye^{22}sa^{2}le^{2}hda^{11}si^2	flip him or her off
u^{22}li^{0}ye^{22}sa^{2}le^{2}hda^{11}ne^{3}hdi^2	for him or her to flip him or her off
da^{2}tsi^{22}ya^{2}li^{11}ye^{22}sa^{2}le^{2}hda^{32}ne^{22}li^2	I'm going to flip him or her off
he^{33}sdi^0 tsi^{22}sgwa^{2}li^{11}ye^{22}sa^{2}le^{2}hda^{11}si^2	Don't flip me off.

12.0 BIBLIOGRAPHY

Feeling, Durbin. 1975. Cherokee-English Dictionary. Tahlequah; Cherokee Nation of Oklahoma.

Mithun, Marianne. 1999. The Languages of Native North America ;
Cambridge : Cambridge University Press

VERB TABLE. INCOMPLETIVE

Prefix	Pronoun		Infix	Root	Root Suffix	Condition	Time	Suffix
	A	B						
y(i^2), i^{22}	g, tsi^{22}	a^{21}gw, a^{21}gi^2	a^{22}d, a^{22}da^{22}, a^{22}da^{22}d		?	-i^{23}si$^{3(2)}$ha^2, -i^{23}si^{32}sg- AGAIN	-a^2, -i^2 PRESENT, IMPER., IMMED.	s, x^{23}tsu^3, x^{3}ke^3, sgo^{21} QUESTION
ts(i^2)	i^{21}n, i^{21}ni^{22}	gi^{2}n, gi^{2}ni^{22}	a^{22}l(i^2), a^{2}li^{11}		h	-i^{23}lo$^{3(2)}$?a^2, -i^{23}lo^{32}sg - REPEAT	-v^{23}?i^2 PAST	sgo^{21}hv^2 BUT IS
w(i^2)	o^{21}sd, o^{21}sdi^{22}	o^{21}gi^{2}n, o^{21}gi^{2}ni^2 ^{2}			s	-do^{3}hdi$^{3(3)}$ha^2, -do^{3}hdi^{32}sg- ACCIDENTAL	-o^{33}?i^2, -o^3?i^2 USUALLY	gwu$^{3(3)}$, wu$^{3(3)}$ JUST/ONLY
n(i^2)	i^{21}d, i^{21}di^{22}	i^{21}g, i^{21}gi^{22}			ts	-o^{23}hv^{3}sga^2, -o^{23}hv^{3}sg- FINISHING	-e^{33}?i^2, -e^3?i^2 RUMOR	le^2 yi^{2}gi^2 OR
d(e^{33})/di^{22}	o^{21}ts, o^{21}tsi^{22}	o^{21}g, o^{21}gi^{22}				-i^{23}do^{32}ha^2, -i^{23}do^{32}h- PLACE-TO-PLACE	-e^{33}sdi^2 WILL BE	dv^{33} DEFINITELY
da^2 (FUT), dv^2 (FUT), da^{2}y (FUT)	h, hi^{22}	ts, tsa^2				-e^{33}ga^2, -e^{33}g- GOING		na^3 HOW ABOUT
d (TOW), da^2 (TOW), dv^{22} (TOW),	sd, sdi^{22}	sd, sdi^{22}				-i^{33}ga^2, -i^{23}hi^{3}h- COME TO DO		hno^{33}, hno^3, hnv^3,

da²y (TOW), di²² (TOW), ts (TOW)							hnv³², AND/ALSO he³³hno³, he³³hn(o³), BECAUSE hye³³hno³, hye³³hn(o³) THEREFORE
di² (AWAY)	i²¹ts, i²¹tsi²²	i²¹ts, i²¹tsi²²				-i⁴⁴di²(ha²), -i²³di³²sg- ABOUT TO	sgi²ni², sgi²n(i²) BUT
i²²x³/i³?	g, a²¹, ga²¹	u²¹, u²¹w				-v²²hv³sga², -v²²hv³sg- TAKING TIME	do²³ka³, ka³, do²³hv³² AINT IT SO?
ga²²		u²¹n, u²¹ni²²			-o³²ga², -o³²g- BECOMING		gi² CLARIFIER
e²²							di⁴⁴na² UNTIL THEN
							yo²¹ GUESSING
							di²³hv³² SO THEN
							e³³ga² CERTAINLY

VERB TABLE. COMPLETIVE STEM

Prefix	Pronoun A	Pronoun B	Infix	Root	Root Suffix	Condition	Time	Suffix
y(i²), i²²	g, tsi²²	a²¹gw, a²¹gi²	a²²d, a²²da²², a²²da²²d		?	-i²³sa³hn- AGAIN	-a², -i² PRESENT, IMPER., sgo²¹ IMMED.	s, x²³tsu³, x³ke³, sgo²¹ QUESTION
ts(i²)	i²¹n, i²¹ni²²	gi²n, gi²ni²²	a²²(i²), a²li¹¹		h	-i²³lo³²ts- REPEAT	-v²³?i² PAST	sgo²¹hv² BUT IS
w(i²)	o²¹sd, o²¹sdi²²	o²¹gi²n, o²¹gi²ni²²				-do³hta²n- ACCIDENTAL	-o³³?i², -o³?i² USUALLY	gwu³(³), wu³(³) JUST/ONLY
n(i²)	i²¹d, i²¹di²²	i²¹g, i²¹gi²²		ts		-o³hn- FINISHING	-e³³?i², -e³?i² RUMOR	le² yi²gi² OR
d(e³³)/di²²	o²¹ts, o²¹tsi²²	o²¹g, o²¹gi²²				-i²³da³²l- PLACE-TO-PLACE	-e³³sdi² WILL BE	dv³³ DEFINITELY
da² (FUT), dv² (FUT), da²y (FUT)	h, hi²²	ts, tsa²				-v³³s- GOING		na³ HOW ABOUT
d (TOW), da² (TOW), dv²² (TOW), da²y (TOW)	sd, sdi²²	sd, sdi²²				-i²³hl- COME TO DO		hno³³, hno³, hnv³, hnv³²

Left form	Variant 1	Variant 2	Form	Meaning
di^{22} (TOW), ts (TOW)			he^{33}hno^3, he^{33}hn(o^3), hye^{33}hno^3, hye^{33}hn(o^3)	AND/ALSO / BECAUSE / THEREFORE
di^2 (AWAY)	i^{21}ts, i^{21}tsi^{22}	i^{21}ts, i^{21}tsi^{22}	sgi^{2}ni^2, sgi^{2}n(i^2)	BUT
i^{22}x^3/i^3?	g, a^{21}, ga^{21}	u^{21}, u^{21}w	-i^{23}di^{32}s-	ABOUT TO
			-v^{22}hn-	TAKING TIME
ga^{22}	u^{21}n, u^{21}ni^{22}		-o^{22}ts-	BECOMING
			do^{23}ka^3, ka^3, do^{23}hv^{32}	AINT IT SO?
e^{22}			gi^2	CLARIFIER
			di^{14}na^2	UNTIL THEN
			yo^{21}	GUESSING
			di^{23}hv^{32}	SO THEN
			e^{33}ga^2	CERTAINLY

VERB TABLE. IMMEDIATE STEM

Prefix	Pronoun A	Pronoun B	Infix	Root	Root Suffix	Condition	Time	Suffix
$y(i^2)$, i^{22}	g, tsi^{22}	$a^{21}gw$, $a^{21}gi^2$	$a^{22}d$, $a^{22}da^{22}$, $a^{22}da^{22}d$		g	$-i^{23}sa^2-$ AGAIN	$-a^2$, $-i^2$ PRESENT, IMPER., IMMED.	s, $x^{23}tsu^3$, x^3ke^3, sgo^{21} QUESTION
$ts(i^2)$	$i^{21}n$, $i^{21}ni^{22}$	gi^2n, gi^2ni^{22}	$a^{22}(i^2)$, $a^{22}da^{22}$, a^2lli^{11}		n	$-i^{22}lo^{23}tsa^2$ REPEAT	$-v^{23}i^2$ PAST	$sgo^{21}hv^2$ BUT IS
$w(i^2)$	$o^{21}sd$, $o^{21}sdi^{22}$	$o^{21}gi^2n$, $o^{21}gi^2ni^{22}$			Ø	$-do^3hda^2$ ACCIDENTAL	$-o^{33}i^2$, $-o^3i^2$ USUALLY	$gwu^3(^3)$, $wu^3(^3)$ JUST/ONLY
$n(i^2)$	$i^{21}d$, $i^{21}di^{22}$	$i^{21}g$, $i^{21}gi^{22}$				$-o^2hna^2$ FINISHING	$-e^{33}i^2$, $-e^3i^2$ RUMOR	$le^2yi^2gi^2$ OR
$d(e^{33})/di^{22}$	$o^{21}ts$, $o^{21}tsi^{22}$	$o^{21}g$, $o^{21}gi^{22}$				$-i^{23}da^2$ PLACE-TO-PLACE	$-e^{33}sdi^2$ WILL BE	dv^{33} DEFINITELY
da^2 (FUT), dv^2 (FUT), da^2y (FUT)	h, hi^{22}	ts, tsa^2				$-e^{33}na^2$, $-u^{11}ga^2$ GOING	na^3 HOW ABOUT	hno^{33}, hno^3, hnv^3, hnv^{32}
d (TOW), da^2 (TOW), dv^{22} (TOW), da^2y (TOW),	sd, sdi^{22}	sd, sdi^{22}				$-i^{22}ga^2$ COME TO DO		

dɪ²² (TOW), ts (TOW)				AND/ALSO he³³hno³, he³³hn(o³), BECAUSE hye³³hno³, hye³³hn(o³) THEREFORE
dɪ² (AWAY)	i²¹ts, i²¹tsi²²	i²¹ts, i²¹tsi²²		sgi²ni², sgi²n(i²) BUT
i²²x³/i³ʔ	g, a²¹, ga²¹	u²¹, u²¹w	-v²²hv¹¹ga² TAKING TIME	do²³ka³, ka³, do²³hv³² AIN'T IT SO?
	u²¹n, u²¹ni²²		-i²²de⁴⁴na² ABOUT TO	
ga²²			-o¹¹gi² BECOMING	gi² CLARIFIER
e²²				dɪ⁴⁴na² UNTIL THEN
				yo²¹ GUESSING
				dɪ²³hv³² SO THEN
				e³³ga² CERTAINLY

VERB TABLE. INFINITIVE STEM

Prefix	Pronoun A	Pronoun B	Infix	Root	Root Suffix	Condition	Time	Suffix
y(i²), i²²	g, tsi²²	a²¹gw, a²¹gi²,	a²²d, a²²da²², a²²da²²d	h		-i²³so³hdi² AGAIN	-a², -i² PRESENT, IMPER., IMMED.	s, x²³tsu³, sgo²¹ QUESTION
ts(i²)	i²¹n, i²¹ni²²	gi²n, gi²ni²²	a²²n, a²²(i²), a²li¹¹			-i²³lo³²sdi² REPEAT	-v²³?i² PAST	sgo²¹hv² BUT IS
w(i²)	o²¹sd, o²¹sdi²²	o²¹gi²n, o²¹gi²ni²²				-do³hdi² ACCIDENTAL	-o³³?i², -o³?i² USUALLY	gwu³(³), wu³(³) JUST/ONLY
n(i²)	i²¹d, i²¹di²²,	i²¹g, i²¹gi²²		s		-o³hv³sdi² FINISHING	-e³³?i², -e³?i² RUMOR	le² yi²gi² OR
d(e³³)/di²²	o²¹ts, o²¹tsi²²	o²¹g, o²¹gi²²				-i²³da³²sdi² PLACE-TO-PLACE	-e³³sdi² WILL BE	dv³³ DEFINITELY
da² (FUT), dv² (FUT), da²y (FUT)	h, hi²²	ts, tsa²				-v³³sdi² GOING		na³ HOW ABOUT
d (TOW), da² (TOW), dv²² (TOW), da²y (TOW),	sd, sdi²²	sd, sdi²²				-i²sdi² COME TO DO		hno³³, hno³, hnv³, hnv³²,

di²² (TOW), ts (TOW)						AND/ALSO he³³hno³, he³³hn(o³), BECAUSE hye³³hno³, hye³³hn(o³) THEREFORE
di² (AWAY)	i²¹ts, i²¹tsi²²	i²¹ts, i²¹tsi²²			-i²²d(vh)di² ABOUT TO	sgi²ni², sgi²n(i²) BUT
i²²x³/i³?	g, a²¹, ga²¹	u²¹, u²¹w			-(v¹¹)hdi TAKING TIME	do²³ka³, ka³, do²³hv³² AINT IT SO?
ga²²		u²¹n, u²¹ni²²			-o¹¹sdi BECOMING	gi² CLARIFIER
e²²						di⁴na² UNTIL THEN
						yo²¹ GUESSING
						di²³hv³² SO THEN
					e³³ga² CERTAINLY	

The Four River Cane Splits Game

nv²hgi² i²hi²²ya² di²²sdlu³²hyv⁴ di²²ne²³hlo⁰do²hdi²³?i²

ᎤᎩ ᎢᎠᏆ ᏗᏍᎦᎥᏅᎢ ᏗᏂᏆᏙᏗ

The game is played by using four river cane sticks about 7 inches long. Each one was split in half lengthwise. Each player threw the sticks up in the air and points were counted based on how the sticks landed.

hi²?a²hnv³ di²²ne²³hlo⁰di² nv²hgi² i²hi²²ya² di²²sdlu³²hyv⁴ di²²gv⁰hdo³hdi² ga²²li⁰kwo²³gi² yu³³si²hta²di¹¹sdi²
lv²htlv⁴ i²²di²²ga²nv²hi⁴⁴dv². sa¹¹gwu³³ha⁴⁴hnv³² di²²sdlu³²hyv⁴ de³³ga²nv²²hi³³sv⁴⁴ di⁴⁴tlv².
di²²ne²²lo⁴⁴hv³sgi²hnv³ da²²sv³hga³lo⁰di²²he³³?i² ga²lv³³la⁰di² wi²du²²de³³ge³³?i² a²le³ da²²na⁰se²hi³he³³?i²
ni²du²²li⁰sta²nv⁴ du²²di³³tsi²²hlv⁴⁴?i². (something long laying plural)

ᎭᏙᎥ ᏗᏂᏆᏗ ᎤᎩ ᎢᎠᏆ ᏗᏍᎤᎦ ᏗᎵᎥᏗ ᏍᏆᎥᎩ ᏔᏍᏆᏴᏗᏍᏗ ᏔᏆᏃ ᏗᎤᏍᎥᎠᏂ. ᏆᏲᏍᎥᏙᎥ ᏗᏍᎤᎦ ᏍᏍᎥᎠᏍᏓ ᏗᏃ. ᏗᏂᏋᏍᏃᎥ ᏆᏗᎡᏍᎦᏗᎢ ᏍᏆᏪᏗ ᎤᏍᏍᏪᎢ Ꮣ ᏆᏙᏍ4ᎠᏗᎢ ᎭᏍᏆᏝᎥ ᏍᏗᏂᏗᎢ.

If all the sticks landed hollow side up, that is 10 points.

   ni²ga⁴⁴dv²hnv³² yi²du²²ho³³hdv²³tsa⁴ (if they fell on their backs) a⁰sgo²³hi² ga²nv³sga²

   ᎭᏍᎪᎥ ᏸᏍᏋᎶᏣ ᎠᏆᎠᏗ ᏍᎥᏆᏍ

If all the sticks landed hollow side down, that is 5 points.

   ni²ga⁴⁴dv²hnv³² yi²du²²ya³hta²nv²³tsa⁴ (if they fell on their faces) hi²sgi² ga²nv³sga²

   ᎭᏍᎪᎥ ᏸᏍᏆᏪᎥᏣ ᎠᏆᎩ ᏍᎥᏆᏍ

2 points for every stick that landed hollow side up

   ta²²li² ga²nv³sga² i²³ga⁴ du²²ho³³dv³³tsv⁴⁴?i²

   ᏪᏓ ᏍᎥᏆᏍ ᏔᏍ ᏍᏋᎶᏣᎢ

1 point for every stick that landed hollow side down.

   sa¹¹gwu³³hnv³ ga²nv³sga² i²³ga⁴ du²²ya³hta²nv³³tsv⁴⁴?i².

   ᏆᏲᏆᎥ ᏍᎥᏆᏍ ᏔᏍ ᏍᏆᏪᎥᏓᎢ

The player with the most points after seven throws wins.

   wu²³go¹¹dv² u²²nv²²hnv⁴ ga²²li⁰kwo²³gi² yi²³di³³di²³nv⁴⁴dv² a²²da²²hlo²²sga².

   ᎤᎠᏟ Ꭴ°Ꭴ-ᎤᎠ ᏍᏆᎥᎩ ᏆᏗᏂᎥᏟ ᎠᏆᏆᏍ

I want to tell you all something I was taught when I was growing up....

go²²hu⁴⁴sdi² a²¹gwa²du²²li³ i²²tsv²²no¹¹se³hdi² ni²ga⁴⁴dv² i²yu⁴⁴sdi² a²¹gwe³³yo²³hnv⁴ tsa²²gwa²tv²si²³di³²sv⁴⁴ʔi²....

ᎯᎦᏂᎵ ᎠᏍᎬ ᎢᏓᏃᏁᎠᎵ ᏂᏍᎤ ᎢᎦᏂᎵ ᎠᏪᎣᏴᎯᏅ ᏣᎾᏎᏴᏴᏗ...

When we lived by the ocean in the East, we followed the Four Mother's Laws but we were still going against one another and we weren't able to come together as one.

na² a²me³³gwo⁴⁴hi²²yu²³lo³hdi² tsi²da²²de²³hv⁴ di²ka²lv³³gv⁴⁴di⁴⁴tlv⁰ ko²²hi⁴⁴gi² tsi²ge²²sv⁴⁴ʔi², nv²hgi² i²²yu³³ni²²tsi² di²ka²no²²wa²dv³³sdi² du²²ni²³hv⁴ tsi²de³³di²²sda³²wa²di³³sv²³ʔi² a²²se³³hnv³ si² tsi²de³³da²²da²le³³gv²³ʔi² a²le³ tsi²²gi²²nu²³lv³hv²sgv² sa¹¹gwu³ yi²ga²²li⁰sdo³hdi²³ʔi².

Ꮎ ᎠᎣᏫᎦᎦᎵ ᎢᏍᏌ ᏗᎠᏝᎬᎵᏢ ᎠᎠᎩ ᎢᎯᏴᎡᎢ, ᎣᎩ ᎢᎦᎯᎢ ᏗᎠᏃᎬᏴᎵ ᏏᏝ ᎢᏍᎵᏴᏣᎵᏴᎡᎢ ᎠᏴᎢᎤ Ꮽ ᎢᏍᏝᏝᎣᎡᎢ ᎠᏓ ᎢᏴᏝᎵᏴᎬᎬ ᏴᎤᏩ ᎠᏍᏝᏴᎠᎢ.

Seven Elders then decided that they needed to ask The Provider for help. One of the Elders went on top of the mountain. When he got there, The Provider told him to build a fire. Then he was told to carry the fire around him in a big circle. After he had done that, the area was cleaned and prepared. Once he had done that, nothing could hit/bother him.

ga²²li⁰kwo²³gi⁰ i²³ya³ni⁴⁴ʔi² a²²ni²²ga²yv⁴⁴li² du²²nu²²go⁰ta²ne³³ʔi² u²²ni²²ta²yo²²hle³³ʔi² u²²ne²³hla³nv²²hi² u²²ni²²sde²²lv⁰hdi²³ʔi². sa¹¹gwu³³hnv³² a²²ga²yv⁴⁴li² u²²sda²tv⁴⁴di⁴⁴tlv⁰ o²²da²lv⁴⁴ʔi² u²²we²²nv³³se³³ʔi². wu²³lu³htsa⁴hno³, u²²ne²³hla³nv²²hi² "ho²²tv¹¹ga²", u²²dv³³hne³³ʔi². u²²ne²³hla³nv²²hi² "a²tsi²³la² yi²wi²hi²hwi²³da² gv²²wa²tu³³hwi²dv², u²³ta³na² ha²de²²ya²ga² hi²do³²gv⁴⁴ʔi²", u²²dv³³hne³³ʔi². u²²sgwa²hdo³hna⁴ sgi² na²²dv³³ne²²hv⁴ u²²da²nv²²ga²lv²³ho³hnv⁴ ge²²se³³ʔi² a²le³ ni²ga⁴⁴dv² u²²dv²²nv³³ʔi⁰sta²no³hnv⁴ ge²²se³³ʔi². sgi²na² nu²²dv³³ne²³la⁴ tla³ go²²hu⁴⁴sdi² u²²yo⁴ gv²²wa⁴⁴ni⁰sdi² yi²ge²²he³³ʔi².

ᏕᎠᎥᎩ ᏔᎯᎢ ᎠᎯᏍᏈ ᏎᏆᎠᎳᏁᎢ Ꭳ°ᎯᎳᎣᎩᎢ ᎤᏁᏪᎣᎯ ᎤᎯᏴᏍᏆᎳᎢ. ᏴᎤᏣ ᎠᏍᏈ ᎤᏴᎵᏴᏈ ᎤᎴᏆᎢ ᎤᏎᎣᏴᏔᎢ. ᎪᎷᏓ, ᎤᎥᎤᎣᎯ "ᎢᏝᎢᏍ", ᎤᏫᏁᎢ. ᎤᏁᏪᎣᎯ "ᎠᎯᏪ ᎠᎦᎠᏲ ᎬᎶᎤᎣᏍ, ᎤᏪᎤ ᎠᎦᏍᏴ ᎠᎥᎬᎢ", ᎤᏫᏁᎢ. ᎤᏴᎢᎥᏉ ᏍᎩ ᎦᎤᏁᏴ Ꭳ°ᎶᎣᏎᏆᎯᎣ ᎢᏴᏓᎢ ᎠᏓ ᏂᏍᎤ ᎤᏫᎣᎢᏔᎤᏫᏃᎣ ᎢᏴᏓᎢ. ᏴᎩᎤ ᏆᏫᎳ Ꮭ ᎠᎯᎦᎵ Ꭴ°Ꭿ ᎬᎯᎯᏍᎵ ᎠᎯᎵᎢᎢ.

On the next night, another Elder went on top of the mountain and on the following night another until all Seven Elders had asked The Provider for help. Each one of the Seven Elders were given a Clan Law.

u²²gi²tsv³³dv²hnv³² u²sv⁴⁴ʔi², so³ʔi² a²²ga²yv⁴⁴li² u²²sda²tv⁴⁴di⁴⁴tlv⁰ o²²da²lv⁴⁴ʔi² u²²we²²nv³³se³³ʔi². ni²²ga⁴⁴ti²³yo³ ni²ga⁴⁴dv² ga²²li⁰kwo²³gi² i²³ya³ni⁴⁴ʔi² u²²ne²³hla³nv²²hi² u²²ni²²ta²yo²²hle²³le³ʔ ge²²tsi²²sde²²lv⁰hdi²³ʔi². si²yv²²wi²³ha⁴⁴ʔi² a²²ni²²ga²yv⁴⁴li² ga²²li⁰kwo²³gi⁰ i²³ya³ni⁴⁴ʔi² yi²³ga³la⁰sda²hli⁴ di²²ka²no²²wa²dv³³sdi² de²²ge³³tsi²²hne²³le³ʔi².

ᎤᏳᏣᏍᏫᏛ ᎤᏍᏔᎡᎢ, ᏍᎢᎢ ᎠᎦᏴᎵ ᎤᏍᏓᏫᏟᏔ ᏙᎳᎿᎢ ᎤᏬᏅᏎᎢᎢ. ᏂᎦᏘᏦ ᏂᏍᎷ ᏕᎵᎤᏳ ᎢᏏᎿᎢ ᎤᎾᏁᏥᎾ ᎤᏂᏔᏳᏍᏆᎵᎢ. ᏍᏆᏇᎢᎢ ᎠᏂᏍᏔᎡᎢ ᏕᎵᎤᏳ ᎢᏏᎿᎢ ᏄᏓᏩᎵᎤ ᏗᎨᏣᏃᏩᏙᎢ ᏕᏏᏂᏓᎢ.

The first Elder was given the Wolf Clan Law.

i²gv²³yi⁴ i²³ga³la⁰sda²hli⁴ ge²²sv⁴ wa²ha²ya⁰ di²²ka²no²²wa²dv³³sdi⁰ da²¹tsi²²hne²³le³ʔi²
ᏔᎡᏦ ᏔᏍᏭᎤᎵᎤ ᏆᏍᎡ ᎦᏫᎶ ᏗᎨᏣᏃᏩᏙᎢ ᏓᏣᏂᏓᎢ

The second was given Blue Clan Law.

ta²ʔli²³ne⁴⁴hnv³ no²³gwu⁰ sa²ho²³ni² di²²ka²no²²wa²dv³³sdi² da²¹tsi²²hne²³le³ʔi²
ᏔᎵᏂᎤ ᏃᏭ ᏍᎭᏥᏂ ᏗᎨᏣᏃᏩᏙᎢ ᏓᏣᏂᏓᎢ

The third was given the Human Clan Law.

tso³ʔi²³ne⁴⁴hnv³ no²³gwu⁰ ki²lo⁴⁴hi² di²²ka²no²²wa²dv³³sdi² da²¹tsi²²hne²³le³ʔi²
ᎧᏔᏂᎤ ᏃᏭ ᎩᎦᎯ ᏗᎨᏣᏃᏩᏙᎢ ᏓᏣᏂᏓᎢ

The fourth was given the Paint Clan Law.

nv²hgi²³ne⁴⁴hnv³ no²³gwu⁰ wo²²di² di²²ka²no²²wa²dv³³sdi⁰ da²¹tsi²²hne²³le³ʔi²
ᎤᎩᏂᎤ ᏃᏭ ᏭᏗ ᏗᎨᏣᏃᏩᏙᎢ ᏓᏣᏂᏓᎢ

The fifth was given the Bird Clan Law.

hi^{2}sgi^{23}ne^{44}hnv^3 no^{23}gwu^0 tsi^{22}sgwa^2 di^{22}ka^{2}no^{22}wa^{2}dv^{33}sdi^0 da^{21}tsi^{22}hne^{23}le^{3}ʔi^2
ᎮᏍᏳᏂᎥ ᏃᎤ ᎯᏍᏆᎥᏗ ᏗᎦᏃᏩᏍᏗ ᏓᏥᏁᎴᎢT

The sixth was given the Deer Clan Law.

su^{23}da^{3}li^{23}ne^{44}hnv^3 no^{23}gwu^0 a^{2}ha^{2}wi^0 di^{22}ka^{2}no^{22}wa^{2}dv^{33}sdi^0 da^{21}tsi^{22}hne^{23}le^{3}ʔi^2
ᏒᏓᎵᏂᎥ ᏃᎤ ᎠᎭᏫ ᏗᎦᏃᏩᏍᏗ ᏓᏥᏁᎴᎢT

The seventh was given the Blind Savannah Clan Law.

ga^{44}li^{0}kwo^{23}gi^{32}ne^{44}hnv^3 no^{23}gwu^0 go^{22}da^{2}ge^{23}wi^2 di^{22}ka^{2}no^{22}wa^{2}dv^{33}sdi^0 da^{21}tsi^{22}hne^{23}le^{3}ʔi^2
ᎦᎵᎪᎩᏂᎥ ᏃᎤ ᎠᏓᎨᏫ ᏗᎦᏃᏩᏍᏗ ᏓᏥᏁᎴᎢT

Now is the time to teach the Seven Clan Laws again. Let's teach them again. We need to teach them again.

a^{2}hna^{33}hnv^{32} na^{11}hi^{2}yu^3 a^{22}da^{22}le^{22}ni^3 ga^{22}li^{0}kwo^{23}gi^2 i^{23}ya^{3}ni^{0}sda^{2}hli^4 di^{22}ka^{2}no^{22}wa^{2}dv^{33}sdi^2 a^{2}le^{22}nv^{0}hdo^{2}hdi^{23}ʔi^2. tsi^{2}do^{33}de^{33}hyo^{22}hv^{11}ga^2. wi^{2}de^{33}di^{22}hyo^{22}hi^{23}so^{3}hdi^2.
ᎠᏃᎾ ᎾᎩᏳ ᎠᏓᎴᏂ ᎦᎵᎪᎩ ᎢᏯᏂᏍᏓᎵ ᏗᎦᏃᏩᏍᏗ ᎠᎴᏅᏙᏗᎢ. ᏥᏙᏕᎰᎥᎦ. ᏫᏕᏗᎰᎯᏐᏗ.

In the beginning the Creator chose the truest, the most kind, and the most good of each of the four kinds of people. The Red Person was sat in the East. The Blue Person was sat in the North. The Black Person was sat in the West, and the Yellow Person was sat in the South. The Creator then gave each person a White Stick and when they held them out toward the center equally they started One Fire.

di²²da²le²²ni²³sgv⁴⁴ʔi², u²²ne²³hla³nv²²hi² du²²su²²ye³³se³³ʔi² wi²du²²yu²²go⁰dv⁴, wu²²da⁴⁴nv⁰hti²³yv⁴, a²le³ wi²da²tse³³tlv⁴ ni²ga⁴⁴dv² nv²hgi² na²²ni³³ʔv⁴ a²²ni²²yv²²wi² ge²²sv⁴⁴ʔi². yv²²wi² gi²³ga³ge⁴⁴ʔi² nv²²do²²gv²³yi⁴di⁴⁴tlv⁰ wa²¹tsi²²ka²hne³³ʔi². yv²²wi² sa²ko²²ni² tsu²²yv²²tlo⁴⁴yi²di⁴⁴tlv⁰ wa²¹tsi²²ka²hne³³ʔi². yv²²wi² gv²³na³ge⁴⁴ʔi² sv²²no³³yi²di⁴⁴tlv⁰ wa²¹tsi²²ka²hne³³ʔi², a²le⁴ yv²²wi² da²lo²²ni² wa²²hi²lv⁴⁴di⁴⁴tlv⁰ wa²¹tsi²²ka²hne³³ʔi². u²²ne²³hla³nv²²hi²hno³² si²²yv²²wi²³ha⁴ ga²²nv⁰sda² u²²ne⁴⁴gv² de²²ge³³tsi²²de³³le³³ʔi² ni²ga⁴⁴dv²hnv³ nv²hgi⁰ i²³ya³ni⁴⁴ʔi² na² ga²²nv⁰sda² a²ye⁴⁴hli⁰ di⁴⁴tlv⁰ wi²du²²na⁰dlo²²hi³sta²ne³³ʔi² si²²ya²tsi²³la² u²²no²²tlv²²hne³³ʔi².

ᏠᏫᏓᎴᏫ, ᎣᎵᎳᏬ-Ꭿ ᏎᏫᎧᏝᏫᏉᎢ ᏆᏚᏯᏆᎢ, ᎵᏞ-ᎿᎡ, Ꮷ ᏆᎸᏙᏢ ᎯᏚᏠ ᏆᎻ ᎠᎯᎡᏪ ᏮᏫᏁᎢ. ᎴᏪ ᎩᏚᏢᎢ Ꮼ-ᎥᎡᏛᎯᏢ ᎬᏲᏫᏓᎢ. ᎴᏪ ᏫᏳᎯᎯ ᏚᎴᎧᏛᎯᏢ ᎬᏲᏫᏓᎢ. ᎴᏪ ᎬᏆᏢᎢ ᏫᎡᏏᏛᎯᏢ ᎬᏲᏫᏓᎢ, Ꮷ ᎴᏪ ᏔᏟᎯ ᎦᎰᏉᎯᏢ ᎬᏲᏫᏓᎢ. ᎣᎵᎳᏬ-ᎠᏃ ᏫᎶᎴᏫᏔ ᏎᎣ-ᏫᎶ ᎣᎵᎡ ᏎᎰᎻᏚᎢ ᎯᏎᎰᎣ- Ꭳ-Ᏼ ᎢᏫᎯᎢ Ꭵ ᏎᎣ-ᏫᎶ ᎠᏜᏓ ᎯᏢ ᏆᏎᎥᏯᏫᏬᏁᎢ ᏫᎶᏫᎮᎳ ᎣᎽᏗᏁᎢ.

Made in the USA
Las Vegas, NV
14 January 2025